WHEN I THINK ABOUT

My Father

Sons and Daughters Remember

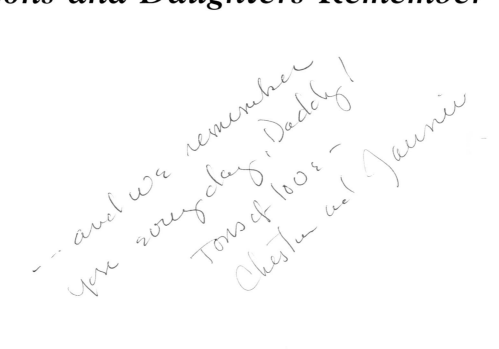

... and we remember
you everyday, Daddy!
Tons of love—
Chester and Jaunin

Edited by Mary Kay Shanley

This book is dedicated to my father George; to Dennis,
who is the father of my children, and to fathers everywhere. —MKS

Special thanks to Paula Granquist, who first saw the need
for a book that celebrates fatherhood.

To create a visual image of fathers, the publisher included graphics in this book
that are neither provided by the essayists nor are intended to be representative of them.

Published by Sta-Kris, Inc., P.O. Box 1131, Marshalltown, IA 50158

Printed by The Kimm Company, Minneapolis, MN

Bound by Musclebound Binding, Minneapolis, MN

ISBN 1-882835-32-8

The text was set in Goudy regular and Goudy italic.

Photos by D.E. Smith

Sally Cooper Smith, Designer

Paul Micich, Creative Consultant

Forward

FATHERS. POWERFUL PEOPLE. Necessary men in the lives of their children, no matter how young or old those children may be.

If they fulfill their role properly, fathers are indispensable. If they are caring, giving, receiving, understanding ... if they encourage freedom and provide structure ... if they father lovingly ... the benefits become immeasurable, and they touch generations not yet born.

Still, a father's influence on a child often goes unrecognized. In fact, many fathers do not realize the importance of their own contributions to a child's development. This book speaks to that importance. It is introspective, perhaps causing one to laugh, cry, think and love.

Isn't that what good fathers do?

By causing children to laugh, cry, think and love, fathers provide the most precious of memories to savor and to celebrate. I have such memories, gifts my father gave me, perhaps unknowingly.

I remember, for instance, standing between my parents in church on Sunday. Second pew from the door. Left-hand side of the aisle. I couldn't see anything except the backs of the people ahead of me. Never saw the altar or the priest. Certainly never understood the sermon. But I didn't wiggle or fuss or talk.

Because I'd struck a deal. "If you're good in church," my father would say, "I'll take you down to the station to watch the train come in."

So after church, my father the postmaster and I would go to the depot. We'd stand on the brick platform, safely away from the tracks, and wait. Even before I could feel the rumble or hear the whistle, my father would lean down. "It's coming!" he'd tell me.

I'd peer down the track until I spied the huge black engine roaring toward us. Whistle screaming. The earth moving. My father's big hand gripping my little one, standing together in anticipation. As the engine passed by, I was frozen.

Then with my hand still inside his powerful grip, I would look up at my father, trying to decide which was more awesome — the train engine or him.

Which is why I wanted to be part of a book celebrating fatherhood.

Mary Kay Shanley

WHAT MORE CAN A FATHER DO, with the hope of it being useful to his son, than provide a living example for him to follow? Mine was born on a New Jersey farm and raised during The Great Depression. He married at age 23, just before the outbreak of hostilities in Europe, and became a schoolteacher because of his love of children and a deeply felt conscientious objection to war.

Dad had an extraordinary gift for encouraging curiosity and self-confidence in children. How clearly I remember one science lesson, part of a unit on the weather, during the year I spent in his fourth grade classroom.

He brought in a rectangular gallon can, recently emptied of turpentine, with a tight-fitting lid. He had the heaviest boy in the class stand on top of the can.

Nothing happened.

Then he poured a small amount of water into the can and heated it on a hot plate. When steam poured from the opening, he used heavy gloves to screw on the cap, placed the can on the desk, and talked about atmospheric pressure and the weight of air. While he spoke, the steam cooled and re-condensed. Finally, 15 pounds of atmospheric pressure acting on every square inch of its top, sides and bottom crushed the can like the jaws of a giant vise.

A spellbound group of 9- and 10-year-olds was convinced they had just been let in on a profound scientific discovery.

Dr. Joseph Hooton Taylor Jr., 55
Professor, Princeton University
Winner of the Nobel Prize for Physics
Princeton, New Jersey
son of Joseph Hooton Taylor

MY DAD WOULD HAVE LIKED ME TO BE A POLICEMAN. He was friends with the cops, as far back as I can remember. By the time I was 3, somebody Dad knew had made me an NYPD uniform. As a kid, I walked the beat with cops. They were always friends with our family.

Dad was a Russian immigrant, a young guy who worked hard, learned the language and loved this place. I think he was one of America's most patriotic citizens. He and Mom bought a bar and grill. It was perfect because he loved people and put jokes into every story. People used to call Dad the Toots Shore of the neighborhood.

When America got into World War II, Dad wanted to enlist but the Army wouldn't take him because he was 40. So he went to work at a defense factory in New Jersey. He died there, of a heart attack.

Three squad cars came to our house with the news. Then, one of the cops took me around that afternoon and talked about how tough it was for a kid to lose a father. I was 10 years old, and that is still the saddest day in my life.

Obviously, I didn't become a cop. The only thing I ever wanted to be was a broadcaster, and I've accomplished everything I set out to. So if there's a heaven, and if my dad's looking down, he'll see that I'm doing what I want. That will make him happy. He was, after all, a happy man.

They say when he died, he was telling a joke.

Larry King, 62
Host of Larry King Live
Washington, D.C.
son of Edward Aaron Zeiger

THE FACE THAT I SAW EVERY DAY in the pages of the Los Angeles *Times* as I was growing up was my father's. From an early age, I took an almost tactile pleasure in the appearance of hot type on newsprint, each letter of his name inscribed deeply and blackly into the surface of the paper.

My father was the daily book critic of the *Times* for more than a quarter century. As a young boy living alone with my mother, the newspaper was a place where I could count on seeing the man whom I encountered in person only on ceremonial occasions.

As I grew older, my father and I drew closer. Eventually, almost miraculously, the day came when I watched my father playing with my 2-year-old son with an easy intimacy that I never knew at that age.

Today, I still have the silver lapel pin that was awarded to my father by the *Times* in recognition of his first five years as a staff writer. And I still have a copy of my father's last book in which he inscribed what turned out to be both a benediction and a bequest:

"To the writer I admire, the son I love, the good man, the warm friend, with hope that he will enjoy and go on to write his own books."

So it is now and forever, as it was in the beginning, that my father manifests himself as a name in print, words on paper, a blessing.

Jonathan Kirsch, 46
Author, book critic and publishing attorney
Los Angeles, California
son of Robert R. Kirsch

THE VOICE OF MY FATHER IS IN HIS LETTERS. Letters arriving weekly that span 25 years of our lives. From a college daughter to a middle-aged married woman settled in Oregon, I still find the good-byes as heart wrenching now as at 21. The letters have lessened the geographic distance from my Iowa home.

My father and I don't travel the information superhighway. We wend along the blue highways, meandering and bending through everyday things like snowfall in November and rain in April and through the big things like the birth of my sister's children and the death of his brother.

Mahler and Mozart, the seasonal swoon of the Dodgers and the Democrats, newspaper articles and family snapshots around Christmas trees fill our letters. The roads we travel are familiar and the course is mapped in detail.

There is an economy of style fitting my father the newspaper man, letters typed and often sent on copy paper. His letters are funny and eloquent, fitting to the Irishman he is with his love of words. And wrapped around these letters are tenderness and love. Always encouraging, always loving, his letters provided comfort to an often homesick daughter.

There is a permanence and truth about letters — about written words. And, it is true that love makes you strong. As my father wrote — it is also true that repetition never dulls the meaning of "I love you."

Rebecca Sonniksen, 48
President, Radius Marketing & Design
Portland, Oregon
daughter of John Knox Craig

MY DAD WAS A QUIET, UNASSUMING MAN. They called him "Chief" at the factory, those men of blue collar or T-shirt. They were quick to jest, often merciless to the little guy or the fat one. But for my dad, "Chief" was said with a genuine smile.

The factory guys remembered Chief had come from a long line of Potawatomi Indian sons who played ball well — baseball, football, basketball. These factory guys were badly prejudiced, too, so it made them feel good to know Chief as one of the guys with whom they could share a job, a smoke, bowling and a beer.

As I came of age in the '60s and sought my Indian roots, I looked down on Dad for never learning the Potawatomi language, philosophy or religion. His later years seemed meaningless as he watched endless ball games on TV through eyes glazed by beer. Never noisy, never mean, just quiet, often chuckling to himself.

My spiritual path, taught by elders wise in the ancient ways, leads us to work hard, be moderate, in harmony and not take ourselves so seriously as to lose our sense of humor.

Dad didn't ever talk of these teachings. In fact, he probably was ignorant of them. He simply *lived* them (except for time spent with his buddy Mr. Hamms from the land of sky blue waters).

As my children graduate from college and embark on careers, they begin as traditional Native Americans yet wise to the present world — bound for successes unimagined. They lack resentment for the dominant society. They lack prejudices. They love to laugh. I now get the long view. It is all about choices. They have the best options and choices.

Tom Topash, 49
Elementary principal
Berrien Center, Michigan
son of Louis L. Topash

MY DAD — and the country's dad for a few years — is the ultimate in leadership, values, integrity and truth. Even when he traveled so much, I always knew he was there, no matter what, the strongest support system that anyone could have.

Dad always listened to me before making a judgment or decision. And he would help me think through things before I had to make an important decision.

He is extremely competitive when it comes to sporting events, in a very healthy way. But he does not like to lose.

He is very thoughtful, practical, kind, loving, intelligent and unselfish. I only hope I have acquired some of his attributes. I only wish everyone could get to know him as I do.

Susan Ford Bales, 38
Public speaker
Tulsa, Oklahoma
daughter of President Gerald R. Ford

My dad started working on the railroad in Oklahoma in 1920. He retired in Ohio in 1962. I don't think he ever earned over $8,000 a year, yet with the exception of a lot and house, he never owed anybody a cent. My dad took out a 20-year mortgage and gave up everything he liked to do to pay the mortgage off in four years.

I use this illustration to show that my dad had the greatest single mindedness of purpose of anybody I know. When he made up his mind that something needed to be done, he put every ounce of effort into seeing that it was done. That is the first of two qualities that come to mind when I think of my dad.

The second is that, without question, he is the most honest person I ever met. My dad had a tremendous responsibility toward his job with the railroad. I couldn't begin to count the number of rainy, cold or snowy nights that I walked through the railroad yard with him, holding a lantern so he could check the seals on boxcars to make sure none had been broken into. I remember him saying to me, "If you are going to accept pay for something, do it right."

My dad passed away on July 20, 1970. There hasn't been a day since that I haven't paused to thank my dad for what he gave me. It always gives me an extra thrill when a player I have coached says he has learned how to work hard by being a basketball player at Indiana University. I'm also pleased when people refer to me as being honest. Such comments are a reflection not on me, but on my dad.

Bob Knight, 55
Teacher/basketball coach at Indiana University
Bloomington, Indiana
son of Carroll Knight

My FATHER'S GREATEST STRENGTH was his ability to present options that caused me to make wise decisions without even knowing I'd been influenced. He also taught me that great opportunities can be missed by reaching hasty conclusions.

In my senior year in high school, Dad came home and said, "How would you like to go to the Harvard-Yale football game next week?"

It seemed like a good thing, so we went to the game. After Harvard lost, Dad suggested we walk through Harvard's famed "yard." He casually asked, "Did you put your application in here?"

He knew darn well that I hadn't. We came from a meager background, and I had been applying to colleges that were close to home, relatively inexpensive and ones I thought I could get into. After all, our school system had all 12 grades in one two-story building.

I jumped to conclusions, saying, "I couldn't get in here! And even if I could, you couldn't afford to keep me here."

To which he replied, "You worry about getting in and *I'll* worry about keeping you in." So I did, and went on to graduate from Harvard College and Harvard Medical School.

Years later, Dad confessed to orchestrating my decision. "I knew if I came right out and said, 'Why don't you apply to Harvard?' you probably wouldn't do it," he told me.

He wanted me to go to Harvard not because I couldn't have gotten a perfectly fine education elsewhere, but because he knew — rightly or wrongly — that the name Harvard would open doors all my life.

And it has.

Dr. James S. Todd, 64
Executive Vice President, American Medical Association
Chicago, Illinois
son of Alexander C. Todd

PROBABLY THE MOST TRAUMATIC DAY OF MY LIFE was when my roommate and I were expelled from boarding school the first week of our senior year. That, for any other parent, would have been the ultimate in disgrace. But my father maintained his sense of humor and even managed to glean a bit of laughter from the headmistress for probably one of the few times in her life.

The punishment my father negotiated with that inflexible woman of power was that my roommate and I were restricted to the school's small campus for the entire year and we were "paroled" the day of our commencement. (My roommate subsequently graduated from Vassar, Number 1 in her class. Suffice it to say that I graduated.)

Years later, I asked Dad what magical influence he had exerted over the headmistress. He responded that he merely asked what her father would have replied had she been dismissed the first week of her senior year. With tears in her eyes, she told my father that her father would have said, "To err is human."

Maddie Levitt, 71
Philanthropist
Des Moines, Iowa
daughter of Ellis Levitt

MY FATHER, ALF LANDON, had a lifelong interest in politics and even became known as the Grand Old Man of the GOP. So obviously, being interested in government and working in local campaigns were some of the givens of my life. Even after Dad no longer held public office, notables of the day continued to stop in Topeka to talk with him. Of course, this was flattering, but Dad loved "talking politics" with anyone who he thought had good sense ... in other words, someone who knew the issues and who could be counted on for a lively debate. What the barber had to say could be just as valid as a cabinet secretary.

Listening in on these conversations was better than any college course. The same was true of family dinners where we discussed events of the day. In matching wits with Dad, my brother and I did not have to agree with him, but we had to be sure of our facts and prepared to defend our views. After coming to Washington, I used to phone home weekly, and Dad and I continued a discussion that had its start at the dinner table years ago.

Dad never hesitated to let me know when he disagreed ... and I still needed to be prepared to defend my votes.

I did not seek office with the intention of carrying on a family tradition. Looking back over the years, following my own star was another quest that Dad began. It may not be a family tradition, but I am proud to be a part of it.

Nancy Landon Kassebaum, 63
Topeka, Kansas, and Washington, D.C.
United States Senator
daughter of Alf Landon

I WAS A SENIOR IN HIGH SCHOOL in the spring of 1974. My political education included the Chicago 7, Watergate and calls for Richard Nixon's resignation. A decade of assassinations had shaken the country. Vietnam War news dominated television, as did photographs in local papers and national magazines. George McGovern ran for president and lost. It was a fertile yet conflict-ridden time. Protests and music were a part of who I was to become and were often the topic of lively conversations at home.

My dad, you see, was the commander of the local American Legion Post.

At Senior Honors Day, when scholarships were announced and school and community awards were presented, my dad came, in uniform, to present the American Legion award to one of my classmates.

My dad was introduced and came to the microphone. He explained that membership in the American Legion was limited to those who served in the armed forces during war time. Pausing briefly, his silence gained everyone's attention. He then said, "It is my prayer that none of you will ever be eligible for membership."

The applause and cheers thundered in the small auditorium.

Two things happened in that moment. First, I realized a sense of pride in my dad unlike any I'd felt before or since. Second, a tumultuous time of rage and confusion for me gave way to a new sense of compassion. It was a definitive moment for me, in which my dad stood center stage and for which I will always be grateful.

The Reverend Glen N. Herrington-Hall, 40
Minister
St. Paul, Minnesota
son of George Herrington Sr.

DADDY IS MY BESSSSSSSSSSSSSST FRIEND! I need him!

Dictated by Andrew Bollard, 3
Chandler, Arizona
son of Paul Bollard

AT THE END OF THE DAY when I go to bed, Daddy tucks me in. We talk together about our day. Daddy wants to know what was the best thing that happened in my day. He wants to know if I was a good friend today. He wants to know if I tried my best today. He reads me a story to help me sleep. We pray together.

That is my favorite part.

Dictated by Amanda Bollard, 6
Chandler, Arizona
daughter of Paul Bollard

MY FATHER HAD A REMARKABLE ABILITY to concentrate on something regardless of what was happening around him. He usually brought scripts, or other business-related reading home on the weekends, and rather than close himself off in a quiet place to read them, he would settle down in his chair in front of our big living room window, which was a very pleasant spot, but was also the center of traffic in our home. Dad thought hallways were a waste of space, so he designed his home without any, except for the bedroom wing. To get to the kitchen from the bedrooms, you had to go through the living room … and there was no "den" or "family room." The living room was where we all hung out, where the TV set was, and my piano.

Dad liked to have his family around him. When my children were small, they spent many weekends at Granny and Grandpa's. They played their games all around him, and sometimes on him, while he did his homework. Often, he would sit outside on the lawn, in a small garden chair, to read. They would construct towers of the light-weight garden furniture over and around him. He would go on reading, seeming to be oblivious of them as they played their games. Only rarely would he admonish them, and then not because of their noise, but because someone had become distressed about something.

We all have many wonderful memories of my father, but I especially cherish this image of him sitting in the midst of my children, he absorbed in his reading and they in their play, but all of them comfortably, cozily aware of each other.

Diane Disney Miller, 62
Vintner
Napa, California
Daughter of Walt Disney

THIS ESSAY IS AS MUCH A TRIBUTE to my mom as it is a remembrance of my dad, because it was through her that I came to know him.

In more myopic moments, I think the purpose of my father's life was to love my mom and bring me into the world. I feel very close to him, despite the fact that we never saw one another. My father was an Air Force bombardier. He was killed by a stray bullet during World War II maneuvers over New Guinea, three months after I was born. One of his last letters to my mom says how much he liked the name Ruth if I was a girl. His letter crossed Mom's in the mail saying how much she liked the name Ann. My name is Ruthanne.

When I think of my dad, I see him as he is in my one and only photo — seated on the back porch steps, ruggedly handsome in his Air Force uniform, reading a letter I always consider as having originated from Mom.

I have frequently thought my father had a greater presence for me in death than he may have had in life. My mom was always quick to say, "Your dad would be proud of you," or, "You're just like your dad." The latter was used to recognize both my strengths and weaknesses, and it served to help me know myself — a mixture of perfectionism, willfulness, social consciousness, conservative on the outside, a rebel on the inside.

I wonder if others who grew up without a parent find it as natural as I. I find it strange that one-parent families are frequently considered sociologically dysfunctional. This is certainly not my perception of my own upbringing.

Thanks, Mom. Thanks, Dad.

Ruthanne Landsness, 53
Health Care Policy Analyst
Madison, Wisconsin
daughter of Donald O. Landsness

My FATHER, Dennis Lee Holm, was killed in Vietnam six weeks before he was due to return home to my mother and me for good. He was shot in the eye by a terrorist while teaching a class. I have no memory of him. I was only 2.

Dear Denny,

At times, I have felt cheated out of the time we should have spent together. I wonder what parts of me are like you, especially since the birth of my son, Simon. Simon doesn't look much like me or my husband, Jose. I wonder if he looks like you did when you were little. I would like to have known you — your likes, dislikes and what made you smile.

When I tell people about you, they say how sorry they are. But I don't want sympathy because I have a dad who has been with me since I was 5. Jay, or Dad as I call him, has always been there for me. When I think of Dad, I think of him. (I know you understand, Denny, because you'd want what's best for me.) He has instilled in me a sense of right and wrong; he's helped me believe I can do whatever I set my sights on. I know he is proud of me.

While you will always be a part of me, Denny, you are where I came from. My dad will always be a part of me, too. He's my beacon, he's where I'm going. He is my guardian angel on earth as you are my guardian angel in heaven. I pray that you will watch over my son, Simon, and all my family until we can meet again.

With love....

Erin Vazquez, 30
Teacher
The Woodlands, Texas
daughter of Dennis Lee Holm and Jay Lawrence Welch

"YOU CAN BE ANYTHING YOU WANT TO BE...."
That's what my dad used to always tell us kids. Well, now that my older brothers and sister are away at college working on that dilemma, I'm home alone with my parents.

One night I had a great idea. I told my dad that I can save him a lot of money. I told him I was planning to work at a fast food chain and at a music store. That way, I could feed myself and also buy all the CDs I wanted, and I wouldn't even have to go to college!

My dad, being ever so clever, said, "Don't you think you should finish the seventh grade first?"

Kenji Miyamoto, 13
Burbank, California
son of Alan T. Miyamoto, M.D.

DAD ALWAYS HAD TIME FOR ME. He seemed to know exactly how much or how little was right for the different stages in a boy's life. *Daddy* knew the names of the Seven Dwarfs and Santa's reindeer. He could build kid-sized cars from cardboard boxes. He was pretty strong because he could lift so many heavy things but I always managed to win when we wrestled on the floor. He made sure I understood that my baby sister and the new puppy were not to be fed out of the same dish.

Dad knew why the fish didn't always bite, how to build snow forts and how to make sure that every 8-year-old in the backyard football game scored a touchdown. He did the driving on August vacations in a station wagon with three kids. And he always managed to find a motel with a pool.

The Old Man came to all of my high school football games. He lent his company car for big dates. He got to like the Doobie Brothers but never warmed up to Pink Floyd. In those peer pressure years, my friends thought my old man was cool.

Today, *Dad* is a friend. We talk business, some politics and lots of fishing. I help him understand the computer; he loans his Bugs Bunny videos to my 5-year-old. I never realized how much he sacrificed until I had a son of my own. I'm hoping to do for him what Dad did for me.

Christopher A. Chase, 36
Marketing Manager
McKinney, Texas
son of David J. Chase

MY FATHER'S NAME was Kee Cly. He was 5'7" tall and a nice man with tan-colored skin. His short brown hair was fading into white hair. He wore a cap all the time.

He was a good father, active, respectful and happy every single day. My father used to smile, laugh, joke around and talk a lot. He never was silent, except if he was working on a vehicle. He used to tease people a lot and he used to like playing games. The way that my father spoke to me was like when your grandparents are teaching you. What I mean is that he used to teach from his talking; of course, all fathers are like that, but he was like God. He used to say not to do this or that.

My father liked riding horses. He knew everything about livestock. My father knew a lot of things. My grandfather, my dad's father, had taught my father many different things. Then, my father taught me so many things just like his father taught him. I sometimes think that all the teaching was from my grandfather.

My dad was an excellent father until someone out there murdered him on August 4, 1995. I never knew someone could be so cruel to a person with a good life, who had kids, and everything. I still think of my father. I wish he were still here with me, teaching me more things.

Kathleen Cly, 17
Mexican Hat, Utah
daughter of Kee Cly

LIFE SEEMED TO HAVE an understandable beginning for me: A person was born and then attended their parents' wedding five years later. That was until a third-grade classmate mocked me for not having a "real" father when I beat her at a game of jacks.

My birth father died when I was 16 months old. My newly-single mother Florence and my Aunt Bess took care of me. And then it seemed that I was thrust suddenly into a new life. This huge, likeable man never went home anymore. My mother, new father and I moved into our own apartment, whereupon Sherman became as real as any father could be.

We forgot that we weren't genetically related. We even looked alike. He took me horseback riding and I learned to box in between flips of his pancakes on Sunday mornings. I admired Sherman for being secure enough in his masculinity to allow my mother to be the one in the family to make financial decisions and wear the tool belt. Yet, from looking at my mother — a Dorothy Lamour look-alike — and my dad — a tough, Bogart type — you would never believe they occasionally traded domestic roles.

I'm grateful to my father for choosing our family and to my mother for taking the risk again.

Now I talk about Sherman to my son, whose birth father chose to leave during my pregnancy. I wish that Spencer could have known his grandfather. Instead, we talk and share pictures and jokes and stories.

When Spencer becomes a father, I hope he has Sherman's qualities. After all, it's not blood that makes a father, but the unconditional love given to a child.

Andrea Engber, 46
Executive Director, National Organization of Single Mothers
Midland, North Carolina
daughter of Sherman Engber

My FATHER WAS BORN in Burlington, North Carolina, in 1890, the seventh in a family of 17, and was self-educated, having completed only the third grade. He read the dictionary to increase his vocabulary and often said that one used profanity or vulgarity to express himself only if his vocabulary were too small. He served 39 years in the U.S. Army and was a veteran of World Wars I and II. He rose from private to full colonel.

He gave me the DNA that molded my mind and body. He taught me by example rather than by rote. He read no books on parenting and nothing about being politically correct, yet he taught me to respect and care about others, to be considerate, honest and to learn. He imparted a sense of humor and a sense of creativity. Courtesy stemmed from discipline and was paramount.

When I decided to pursue medicine instead of following in his footsteps, his disappointment was great but concealed. First, he apologized for not having the means to send me to medical school, then said he would be my biggest booster.

He was.

I have emulated him without knowing it.

I am my father's DNA messenger and his biggest booster, as he was mine.

Charles Clinton Griffin Jr., 74
Retired physician
Randleman, North Carolina
son of Charles Clinton Griffin

MY FATHER WAS 52 WHEN I WAS BORN. I never thought of him as being older than other fathers; I just knew he was very special because he fought in WWI rather than WWII like everyone else's father.

He was a wheat farmer who wore long-sleeved shirts and khaki pants with cowboy boots and a Stetson every day of his life. Daddy (you don't mind, do you?) was handsome, a dark tan face except for his snow-white forehead. He only finished eighth grade, but he was famous.

Everyone in town knew more about Daddy than I ever would. Like why his name was Dugan. They called him that, but have forgotten why or won't tell. He was famous for being "tight." His nickel is still taped to the Justice Rexall Drug mirror behind the soda fountain. Daddy used it to buy someone a cup of coffee once.

He was famous because he had an article written about him in the *Wichita Falls Record Times*. He found and returned a wallet with several hundred dollars in it. The man lost his wallet while changing a tire on the highway and it blew into Daddy's wheat field where he plowed it up a year later. During the time he was looking for the owner, Daddy lost his entire crop to hail and had to borrow money to plant again. The reporters liked the story. AP picked it up.

From Daddy, I learned about honesty, hard work, being good and how to wave by raising your index finger from the steering wheel of the pickup truck. Bouncing along, he taught me the only song he ever knew, "Take Me Out to the Ballgame," even though we never saw one.

Folks elected him mayor twice, even though he never ran or even filed for office. My daddy was famous. Ask anyone in Chillicothe, Texas.

Mary Jane Davis Holm, 51
Development Director
Houston, Texas
daughter of K.G. Davis

CAN YOU IMAGINE growing up in a house full of the most loved cartoon characters in the world? Can you imagine talking with Bugs Bunny, Porky Pig and Daffy Duck at breakfast over a bowl of Cheerios; sharing lunch with Yosemite, Foghorn and Woody Woodpecker, and eating supper with Sylvester and Tweety???

No kid could dream up these scenarios, but I lived them. My mom gave moral support to this menagerie, and in between sleeping and homework, I sat around all day and laughed.

I didn't need TVs, CDs or even MDs. All I needed was my dad, Mel Blanc. Laughter was always the best medicine for me.

Still, I was a bit of a pest. I wouldn't let my pop relax. He was always on a constant audition, creating new voices for characters I would dream up or find in the newspaper or comic books. And, after school, all the neighborhood kids would congregate at my house to hear these characters come to life. My dad had no rest.....but he loved it.

My pop was probably the most versatile voice artist who ever lived. He was responsible for creating more than 600 cartoon character voices. He sold more than 14 million albums for Capitol Records. And during the heyday of radio, he appeared in 18 network shows a week including Jack Benny, Burns and Allen, and his own Mel Blanc Show.

Every day, my dad is heard by more than 200 million people, making his voice the most heard voice on this planet for the last 50 years.

What a dad I had!

Noel Blanc, 57
TV, motion picture producer and voice artist
Beverly Hills, California
son of Mel Blanc

I LOVE MY DAD because he spends time with me. I like to wrestle with him and sleep in the tent in the family room with him.

Eric Spilky, 4
Albert Lea, Minnesota
son of Richard Spilky

WHENEVER I SEE AN EGG, I am reminded of the only spanking I received from my father. As a child, my daily job on our farm in South Dakota was to gather the eggs and crate them so they could be taken to the market and traded for food. Each evening at dinner, my father would ask, "How many eggs today, Johnny?" I was always able to report a rather constant number.

Eventually, the task became boring and tedious. So I stopped gathering the eggs but daily reported some fictitious number I might have gathered had I bothered to collect them. I failed to take into account that there would be no eggs to take to the market at the end of the week. Besides, my father fed the chickens each morning and was able to see that no eggs had been gathered for several days.

When my father finally confronted my duplicitous behavior, he calmly told me that lying would not be tolerated and I would be punished. I was, but only after the painful uncertainty of waiting more than a week for the unknown moment.

When it came, the encounter was clearly more difficult for this gentle man than for me. For our family, love was never an abstract notion. It was beautifully modeled in the life of this spiritual giant. His powerful influence lives on in the lives of all who knew him.

Dr. John M. Schaeffer, 58
Minister
Billings, Montana
son of William J. Schaeffer

My FATHER WAS A SMALL, SERIOUS-MINDED MAN who was always called Father. I grew up at a time when fathers and children weren't particularly close, his primary concern being to provide for his family, now and hereafter.

I would spend time with him on winter trips by horse-drawn bobsled to cut ice from the river. Such "ice bees" with neighbors were a break from the routine and a chance to see some of the "outside world." It was during those trips that my father would talk about what was expected of me as I got older.

He had strong ideas of right and wrong. They probably came from his own pious German-immigrant father who once whipped him for climbing an apple tree on Sunday. Grandfather and a brother were our township's first homesteaders in 1869 and he helped found a pioneer church. He passed his devotion to honesty and integrity on to my father, along with opinions of such evils as strong drink, cards and dancing.

My parents married young, worked hard and taught us to do the same. Father liked farming and was able to buy 400 acres before he became ill with cancer at age 60. He died at home, two pain-filled years later.

I have lived a quarter of a century longer than he. I have played some cards and enjoyed a bit of wine, but I never learned to dance and it still bothers me when a son sometimes insists on Sunday field work. Some things have changed, but Father's honesty and integrity still influence my life and, I hope, those of my children and grandchildren.

Melvin G. Dorr, 88
Farmer
Marcus, Iowa
son of Fred L. Dorr

I WAS 5 YEARS OLD WHEN MY MOTHER DIED. My father was only 40. The day after my mother's funeral, he locked himself in his bedroom. The door had to be broken three days later to get him out. He grieved for her till his last breath when he left this world at 87.

Life with father is my vivid memory of everyday life at home, where he remained after I left India 50 years ago. He did not marry again in spite of pressure from my grandmother, five uncles and four aunts. His answer was always the same: "I cannot take a chance putting my children in the hands of a stepmother."

In our joint family of 65 members living together under one roof, we were 12 cousins growing up together. My father and uncles had equal right to discipline any of us. One day for doing something naughty, I was spanked by an uncle in the presence of my father. My father had not even so much as called me a naughty boy ever, for in his eyes I could do no wrong. He took me to his room after my punishment. Taking me on his lap, he said, "If anyone punishes you, it hurts me so so much." Tears were rolling down his face.

Stories of such love are too numerous to recount. My children know the place they occupy in my heart. They also understand why my father has a very special place inside me.

Romen Basu, 72
Author, publisher
New York, New York
son of Suren Basu

HI. I'M JOHN. I am 12 years old and have a father named David who is 32 years old. My father and I do not have a good relationship because my parents are divorced. I try everything to do to see him but it just doesn't work. The only time I can see him is if he goes to my grandma's house whenever I am there.

My parents left each other when I was about 4 years old. Ever since, my father never gave me anything but a skateboard. When I lived with my grandma, I was happy because I was able to see my father every morning. I love my father and he loves me.

But the way he can prove that is if he would at least try to see me and my big sister. I hope one of these days I can move in with my dad and live with him until I am 18 years old. But if this cannot happen, I would at least want to see him every weekend and summer.

But as much as I know he loves me, it really doesn't matter what he does because I love him, too.

John David Barrera Jr., 12
Houston, Texas
son of John David Barrera

WHEN I WAS 10, my parents separated. My father took my sister and me to Kentucky; my mother took the others to California. Over the next few years, I became very close to my father. I remember him often saying, "Son, whatever you do, always put forth your best effort."

After my thirteenth birthday, my father introduced me to the working world as a furniture refinisher helper. He taught me to save and manage money. Every Sunday, the three of us went to church. My father was the deacon.

Just when I thought I was on top of the world, my father gave me the shocking news that he and my mother decided to work their problems out and we would be moving to California. I felt that he should have considered my feelings.

After that, I drifted away from my father. Everything he taught me, I'd do the opposite. I started using drugs and ended up in prison. My father was there for me, not once turning his back. When I was paroled, he gave me a home placement and found me a job. After being released, he brought my clothing and gave me his automobile.

But one thing led to another, and after life on the run, I ended up back in prison, serving a life term. When my father became very sick, his only wish was to see his youngest son. That never happened. Finally, in 1994, I took a picture and sent it to him. My sister said after he got the picture and read the letter, he was full of joy.

The next day he passed away with my picture in his hands. They buried him with the picture.

Frederick D. Jones Sr., 43
Inmate, William E. Donaldson Correctional Facility
Bessemer, Alabama
son of William L. Daniels

I am an expert expert. I know a lot about fatherhood because my father is a real hood. He makes his living drawing cartoons about me and Dolly, Jeffy, PJ and our Mom. People think Daddy is kind and loving, but the truth is he has been exploiting his whole family for years, including Grandma! We have no secrets. Nothing is private. Everything that happens in our house appears in "The Family Circus" which runs in our local paper and most of the stuff in another out-of-town newspaper. And I think what really burns me up is I have to take over the cartoon every so often and save it with my own great drawings and I don't even get a raise in my allowance! I am thankful that at last the truth is out. **Billy**

P.S. He doesn't even know how to spell his first name ~~tite~~ ~~write~~ right!

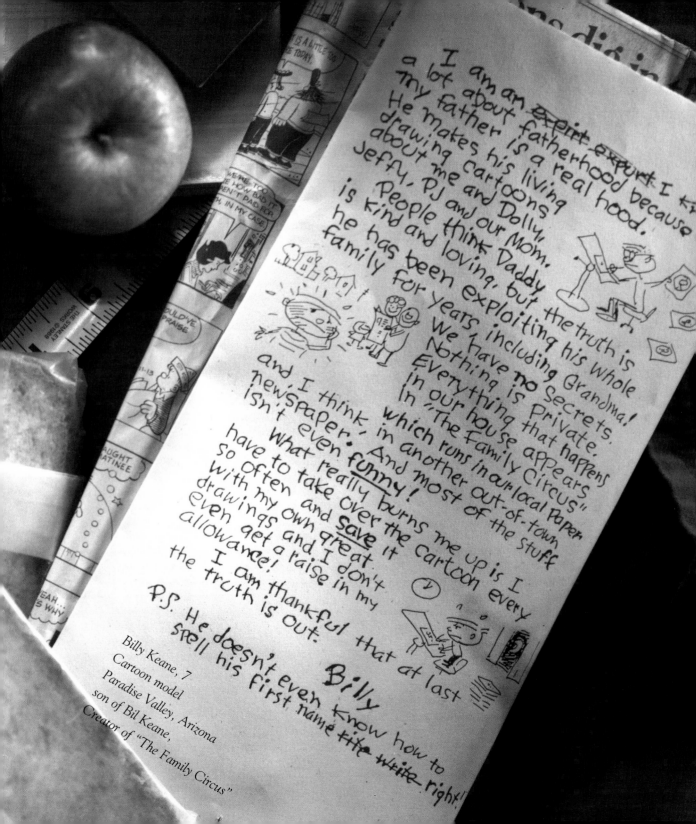

Billy Keane, 7
Cartoon model
Paradise Valley, Arizona
son of Bil Keane,
Creator of "The Family Circus"

My PARENTS WERE MARRIED in 1932 at my grandfather's fish camp on Lake of the Woods. The next spring, they loaded their belongings onto my dad's boat and moved to Buffalo Point, Manitoba. In the summer, they lived in a cabin Dad built. He fished Buffalo Bay, setting 10,000 feet of nets, lifting and resetting them daily. In the winter, they rented a house in town. Some days, Dad walked five or six miles to cut pulp. Other days, he'd walk 20 miles to check his trap line. On more than one occasion, he would spend the night in 30 below weather, building a fire to keep warm.

Though neither rich nor educated, my dad cared for all nine of us, teaching us to work hard and appreciate what we had. We knew everything was attainable, if only we had courage to pursue it.

His work ethic carried me to my goals: winning a Silver Medal in the Winter Olympic Games in 1972 and playing for the Detroit Red Wings of the National Hockey League.

Henry Boucha, 44
Counselor
Warroad, Minnesota
son of George Boucha

DADDY IS WHAT I CALL HIM. Daddy works hard at school helping kids. He works hard at hockey, too. He is my coach and helps me to be a better hockey player and helps other players on my team, too. He is the Mites coach.

Daddy wants me to be a nice boy and grow up right. Daddy takes me hunting and fishing; in the winter we go ice fishing. We go houseboating and we explore the islands and look for eagle feathers and old Indian stuff like arrowheads and pots. It is hard. I love my daddy because he loves me and takes care of me.

Jean Paul Boucha, 7
Warroad, Minnesota
son of Henry Boucha

I'M NOT SURE WHEN I LIT MY FIRST MATCH, but there was a certain fascination in seeing the flame, then the smoke when the flame was blown out. Playing with matches came first, followed by cigarettes. As best I remember, the age was 9 and my cohort was my neighbor, age 7. The location was the large drainage pipe under the road, connecting a creek on either side. We could light matches, puff on cigarettes and cough to our hearts' delight on our way to manhood.

One day, while I was enjoying a smoke in the privacy of the drainage pipe, my older sister looked into the creek, saw smoke coming from the pipe and promptly reported to my father that: 1) Eddie was last seen going in the drainage pipe, and 2) smoke was coming out of the pipe. Older sisters have a way of blunting a brother's quest for manhood.

My father was not only a smoker but a "yeller." Short, heavy-set, German-Swiss. If his booming voice didn't command attention, his tyrannical look did. The combination was awesome.

That evening, he called me into the front room and asked matter-of-factly if I would care for a cigarette. Recognizing pending doom, I remained silent and looked at anything but his eyes. I knew the clap of thunder that was his voice was about to descend. I waited for what seemed like an hour before he said, "If you are going to smoke, please do it in the house where there are ashtrays." His voice was understanding, his eyes anything but fierce.

In the intervening smoke-free years, his message and its delivery are always with me. Thanks, Dad, for recognizing that important messages require a special presentation.

Edward Greub, 61
Real estate appraiser
San Francisco, California
son of Edward J. Greub

As a businesswoman in the stock market, I am influenced by the popular notion that hoarding wealth is of the utmost importance in life. I increasingly find myself relying on my role model — my father — to remind me that there is a *giving* side to life as well.

While making a good living in Corporate America, my father has always found the time to leave the office and walk to the local shelter to serve hot lunches. He has kept a watchful eye on several homeless people through the years — quietly dropping off coats to them when the weather turns cold and leaving a hot meal.

Although I sometimes kid my father for having planter boxes full of geraniums outside his San Francisco office window and bushels of wheat and a garden hoe as adornments in his executive office, I respect him for being bold enough to go against the grain of big business and power lunches. He instead utilizes his time to make statements of peace and give back to the community and the environment in which he lives.

Never by preaching, but through acts of kindness, my father has subtly influenced his community to make positive changes. Each time I return to San Francisco for a visit, I see more offices with tiny planter boxes outside their windows.

Suzanne Greub, 32
Institutional Equity Sales
Chicago, Illinois
daughter of Edward Greub

MY FATHER WAS AN ADVENTURER. Throughout my childhood, I remember my father saying that there really are only two kinds of people in this world: those who take risks and those who avoid them. Not gambles, he would say, but calculated risks. Indeed, when I was older, he recounted to me painful memories of his own father gambling away the family's modest resources during The Great Depression by betting on the horses. Rather than this making him risk adverse, it led him to moderate his own penchant for risk taking through careful analysis of the potential benefits and costs.

But in the end, it was the risk that excited him.

It was also the risk that rewarded him.

Many people retire reflecting upon the paths they did not choose, always staying on the safe and familiar. Not my dad. In his lifetime, he has published an entertainment magazine, directed a computer consulting firm, co-owned a trucking company, taught at a university, authored a book on entrepreneurship, been president of a college board of trustees and — my personal favorite as a child — owned several candy companies.

Even today, at age 70, he is busy writing a book on how *not* to retire and a second on the differences between liberals and conservatives.

Does he have any regrets? Maybe some. But not over paths not taken. He took them all. And along the way, he taught me to be an adventurer, too.

Wade F. Horn, PhD, 41
Director, The National Fatherhood Initiative
Lancaster, Pennsylvania
son of John D. Horn

MY FATHER WAS NOT MY ROLE MODEL. He coughed every morning; I never smoked. He came home too late some nights; I never drank. He had "business friends" with whom the friendship lasted only as long as the business relationship. I never wanted to be a businessman.

Still, people tell me how much we are alike. We love to tell jokes and stories. We take great joy in our friends (although he has outlived almost all of his). I once saw a quiz that asked, "What was the first car that Morgan Freeman drove in the film *Driving Miss Daisy?*" When I asked my father, at age 87, four years after he saw the movie, he replied, "It was a Hudson, wasn't it?" It was. My memory's excellent; his is probably better.

We both shared the same major shortcoming — too often, we found our friends more alluring than our family. For my father, this was compounded by his frequent, long business trips.

Yet at 91, he now feeds my mother twice a day as she languishes in a nursing home. He does her laundry. He says that she raised the children; now it is his turn to take care of her. As a young man, he had to do the same domestic duties as his mother slipped into insanity. He never complains. He grows kinder each year.

I started out trying to avoid his little vices. Now, I hope that I can emulate his large virtues for the rest of my life.

Bob Nordvall, 56
College administrator
Gettysburg, Pennsylvania
son of Stuart Nordvall

My father provided us with two invaluable things.

The first was a deep and abiding feeling of being loved. Ours was an immigrant-oriented family. The words "I love you" were used sparingly. Additionally, Dads didn't spend a lot of time with their children during The Depression and thereafter because they were too busy making a living. But by his behavior, Dad communicated that, next to our mom, we were the world to him.

The second thing was a sense of being safe. We grew up in a world which was filled with discrimination, alienation and violence. Dad told us so. As a boy, I did not know if people were more angry at us for being Catholic or being German. All I knew was they sure were angry. But we had a sense that our father was there to protect us. I had no doubt he would lay down his life for us kids.

As a result of feeling loved and safe as a boy, I felt loved enough and safe enough as an adolescent to explore the world with confidence. I didn't need to seek love or safety in the wrong places. I was an apprentice to my father who taught me how to be a man, how to stand tall and not be afraid. So when I became a man, I knew my job was to provide love and protection to the little ones of this world who are in danger.

If anyone ever wanted to know why I so love being the keeper of Father Flanagan's dreams, go back and look at the security and safety which were the hallmark of my childhood.

Father Val J. Peter, 61
Executive Director, Father Flanagan's Boys' Home
Boys Town, Nebraska
son of Carl J. Peter

WELCOME TO THIS SIN-SICK WORLD *and the challenge you have to walk in your daddy's footsteps,* read the telegram which arrived when I was born.

Daddy, of course, was the Reverend Billy Graham. Though he was already famous by the time I arrived, the course of my early life is better described as infamous. Rather than rising above *this sin-sick world,* I sunk into its mire of pleasure-seeking self-centeredness. The world was my playground, and I played hard.

By the time I was 21, I had drunk deeply from the world's cup of amusements, but I was empty. On my twenty-second birthday, my father said to me, "Franklin, there's a struggle going on in your life. You're going to have to make a choice either to accept Christ or reject Him."

His words made me angry, but I knew he was right. Soon afterwards, I came to terms with the truth that I, like everyone else, was a sinner who needed God's forgiveness. I asked Jesus Christ, who died on the cross for our sins and rose from the grave, to be my Savior and Lord.

Today, I am committed to walking in a new set of footsteps — not my own and not even my earthly father's, but my Heavenly Father's. The path leads into some of the world's most desperate regions where, through the Christian relief organization Samaritan's Purse, we offer hurting people both physical and spiritual help. Life's full, and I'll always be grateful that Daddy challenged me to follow Christ.

Franklin Graham, 43
President, Samaritan's Purse
Boone, North Carolina
son of the Reverend Billy Graham

YOU HAVE TURNED CORNERS that are forever gone;
Born into a wilderness
Of hopes, meager. In a past,
Too long remembered and retold.
Your father, always winning
Old battles in lost wars.
His fiddle always primed for the dance.
You were for work;
Now at ninety-six you say
When asked how your eyesight is:
"Every day is a little darker. But it's not so bad.
Most of the people I would like to see
Would not look as good as they did when
      I last saw them.
But I would like to see how
      the cattle are doing."

Gene McCarthy, 79
Poet and former U.S. Senator
Woodville, Virginia
son of Michael McCarthy

FIVE THINGS YOU MIGHT WANT TO KNOW About My Father:

1. We look alike. Like most girls, I was told when I was growing up I looked like my mother. Wrong. Now looking in the mirror, I see the shape of my father's face, his eyebrows, his blue eyes. Once when I was about 12, I met a man, a friend of my father's, who said, "You are exactly your father's daughter; I would have known you anywhere." Now I know, that man was right.

2. My father's life was a success story. He left school when he was 13 and went to work. He got better and better jobs because, I'm sure, he was hard working, personable, thrifty. He opened his own business with two partners and was successful. Yet he never made much of his own success, acted like it was just what he was supposed to do — and I believe he thought it was.

3. He met my mother on a subway train. He went home and told his mother he had met the girl he was going to marry and she had red hair. His mother said her hair was probably dyed. On the subway he had met a redhead as acerbic as his mother. And married her.

4. He is a nice guy. He would come home every night for dinner at six. He would send me to the college I wanted to go to. He was always consistent and reliable and made me expect men to be that way. Because of the way he was, I married a decent man.

5. He will be 90 soon. He still looks at least 10 years younger, still is amazingly shrewd and sharp. When he had a small stroke a year ago, he drove himself to the hospital. He has trouble sleeping and roams about the apartment all night. If he looks back on his life, I would think he does it without any great sense of pride but without any guilt or regrets and that, for him, would be just as good.

Myrna Blyth
Editor-in-Chief & Publishing Director, Ladies' Home Journal
New York, New York
daughter of Benjamin Greenstein

"DWAINE, TELEPHONE. It's your dad...."

Being struck by lightning was more likely.

The conversation was trivial, but when you haven't spoken to a parent in 22 years, where do you start? My father interrupted, saying he could tell I didn't want to talk. Then he hung up.

It would be another 16 years before I'd hear from him again. Now a father myself, I'd put the anger behind me. (How can you be angry at a shadow?) I'd been told he had another child, but learned it was a niece. His only grandchild was my daughter. And he wasn't going to miss out being her "papa."

A rendezvous was arranged. I was finally going to look into the eyes of my father. I only hoped hidden feelings wouldn't surface and make me want to deck him. After all, I owed him my life and the opportunity to be a father.

"Dwaine," my mother said, "this is your daddy." We locked looks. His health had whittled him to 125 pounds, but I could see me in him and wondered what else I was made of that I hadn't considered.

In the end, I helped plan his funeral. It was then that I learned he'd been a career soldier. I guess devoting your life to a substitute family helps fill a void, though I never knew if not being part of my life was a void he wanted to fill. Still, I think our time together gave him what he had lost out on for so long.

And as for me? I *never* not want to be there for my daughter.

Dwaine R. Simms, 45
MELD for Young Dads Program
Minneapolis, Minnesota
son of Oscar Eugene "Calvin" Simms

I'M HAPPY WINDSURFING with Dad fast on the Cape. We fall in the water — boom! But I can windsurf all by myself. Dad helps me. I push Dad in backwards and he backflips.

My favorite sport is baseball. Dad helps me hit the ball. I love to hit the ball with people from church. I like to slide into second base — boom! Dad made me a walker. We make believe I'm playing baseball. I run to first, second, third and home.

Dad is my buddy.

Josh Lilley, 10, who lives with cerebral palsy
Acton, Massachusetts
son of the Reverend Ross Lilley

MY FATHER GAVE ME THE FOREST. On weekdays, he toiled long hours at the synagogue. But every Saturday afternoon, after Shabbat services, he would come home early to take my brother and me for a walk in the woods behind our house.

We hiked along Turkeycock Run, past silver stands of beech trees and bunkers dug by Union soldiers during the Civil War. Like Shakespeare, Dad constantly discovered sermons in stones, and books in the running brooks. As we strolled, he shared the stories of his week and listened to ours. He taught us the names of wild flowers, the call of geese, the sweet smell of sassafras root. Dad showed me how to read landscape like Torah, a sacred scroll. As we walked, the holy letters leaped forth from snakes' scales and dragonfly wings and became poetry.

Over the years, I have traveled far from that familiar woodlot. I have hiked the deciduous uplands of Northern Kentucky, camped beneath the last virgin hemlocks in the Shenandoah Valley, and wandered along the riparian band of cottonwood and willow that lines the Missouri River's banks. Along the way, I followed in my father's footsteps and became a rabbi. Now I live in Idaho, where I teach Torah and walk with my daughters in the ponderosa pine forest that wraps the northern Rockies like a green mantle.

Yet wherever my journeys have taken me, I have felt my father's presence and treasured his incomparable gift. When God's green earth speaks to me, it is in Dad's voice. Comforting. Brave. Wise.

Dan Fink, 35
Rabbi
Boise, Idaho
son of Arnold Fink

I REMEMBER MY FATHER, a little man sitting at a big desk (now mine!) surrounded by mountains of books, in shelves from floor to ceiling. I wondered: Did he read them all?

More than a rabbi, he was an indefatigable messenger of good will, the community beacon who taught Jew and Christian, Pole and Irish, black and white how to live together. Every Sunday I would sit in a corner of a radio studio while he broadcast *The Humanitarian Hour*, an analysis of the events of the day illuminated through his universalism, optimism and hope. His conviction that human beings are intrinsically decent, that rational thought can solve all problems infused my being. Now, in a darker time when reason has been largely dethroned and intergroup tensions exacerbated, that belief still inspires my thinking and bolsters my spirit.

Dad was the great storyteller, chuckling at his own jokes, able to grasp life through anecdote. He could take the abstract and make it concrete, the profound and make it simple. It was a great gift — which I now see in my son.

Most of all, it is not the public image but the private father whom I remember and cherish. The aroma of his after shave lotion, the feel of his whiskers against my face are still with me. And in the summer, when the days were long and Buffalo was warm, I would say, "How about throwing the ball?" He never was the one to say, "Enough! Let's quit."

The arc of the baseball from father to son formed the invisible cord that binds us still.

Arnold G. Fink, 60
Rabbi
Alexandria, Virginia
son of Joseph L. Fink

RECOLLECTIONS OF MY FATHER probably can be summed up in one word: aviation. World-famous flyers, friends or acquaintances of Dad's were an integral part of my growing up. Dad made his first flight in 1918 and jumped in a self-packed parachute in 1920. He trained fighter pilots in World War I and was an aide to General Billy Mitchell.

Dad was the first American businessman to fly his own company plane abroad. And it was in this very plane, a Lockheed Vega, that I experienced my first ride into the wild blue yonder, with Dad at the throttle.

I grew up in awe of his accomplishments.

Considering who my father was, it came as no surprise that I should graduate from West Point and earn my wings in the U.S. Air Force. Nor that one day we would share the same sky, flying in formation.

But what did surprise us — what we hadn't anticipated — was the transfer of that sense of "awe." Now, it was my father who marveled over what I was able to accomplish. We learned that being blessed by the good fortune of achievement, that being widely acclaimed, imposes a burden on those who come before as well as on the person who's been blessed.

I'm also surprised — and pleased — to find that my enthusiasm for space is as intense as ever. The creativity I'm experiencing now is not something my father enjoyed when he was this age. I've learned to build on the past but not to be dependent upon it.

That is a lesson I wish to pass on.

Dr. Buzz Aldrin, 66
Moonwalker – first landing on the moon –
and science fiction author
Emerald Bay, California
son of Edwin Eugene Aldrin

AFTER THREE YEARS OF TEACHING IN AFRICA, I moved back home to Greenfield Center. A father myself now, the old distance between my dad and me grew smaller. We both loved the Adirondacks and went fishing together. One August day, on Deer Pond, three loons landed nearby. Something happened then few ever see. Flapping their wings and calling, those loons began running across the lake.

"They're dancing," my father said. As he said it, the trout started biting. We pulled in fish after fish, loons dancing around us.

Twelve years later, my father suffered a heart attack while having a check-up. It took several minutes to resuscitate him. Afterwards, he called me to his side in the hospital.

"I was gone," he said. "I looked down and saw my body on the table. Then I began to see things, only instead of seeing them, I was there. I saw Mr. Pray. He was Huron Indian — my first partner. Things were really good there," he said. "Plenty of hunting and fishing. He'd been waiting for me. Then I was back in that boat with you on Deer Pond. The loons were dancing, the trout pulling our lines.

"I could have stayed there," he said, "but I still had things to do." He squeezed my hand again. "Had to come back and tell you, you don't need to be afraid of dying."

I nodded, my eyes full of tears, and he smiled.

"Just remember how those loons danced," he said.

Joseph Bruchac III, 53
Writer/storyteller
Greenfield Center, New York
son of Joseph Bruchac Jr.

DAD WAS A CONSUMMATE FLY FISHERMAN. He sought trout on meandering streams in northern Wisconsin, teased largemouth bass with homemade poppers in the glassy bays of Wood Lake, and caught countless bluegills on barbless flies laid silently and expertly across a spawning bed.

When Dad fished, his pipe wagged to one side of his mouth and a smile of pure bliss lit his face. We all learned to wet a line from him. Mom was his first student. She followed him along the grassy shoulders of trout streams before we were born.

When my brother and I first began flailing our rods to and fro, Dad would say, "You'll never catch fish in the air." We'd watch in awe as he sailed a line into a tiny pocket between the reeds. Determined to do the same, we'd draw double the line we could handle. It ended up puddled at our feet or piled in a pathetic knot on the water.

Not long before he died, Dad taught his youngest grandchild the same lessons on the same lake with the same patience. His admonitions and bits of encouragement echoed through the past, mingling with the smell of Wood Lake in springtime. My 10-year-old daughter listened intently to a litany of instructions and then proceeded to flail her rod to and fro.

"You'll never catch fish in the air..."

Maybe not. But one couldn't help but catch love from a fly fishing lesson taught by Dad.

Cris Peterson, 43
Dairy farmer, writer
Grantsburg, Wisconsin
daughter of Bill Hoeppner

WHEN I THINK ABOUT MY FATHER...